PLAYALONG
CELLO
Christmas tunes

Easy cello
with piano
accompaniment

plus CD demonstration
and backing tracks

Arranged by David Gedge

Bosworth
8/9 Frith Street
London W1V 5TZ

This book © Copyright 1999 Chester Music.
Order No. BOE005015 ISMN M-2016-4038-9

Music processed by New Notations
Cover design by Ian Butterworth
Printed in Great Britain by Printwise (Haverhill) Limited, Suffolk.

CD orchestrations and production by Paul Honey
Solo cello: Justin Pearson

Unauthorised reproduction of any part of this publication by any means
including photocopying is an infringement of copyright.

Contents

Rise Up Shepherd
4

Away In A Manger
6

Mistletoe And Wine
8

O Christmas Tree
10

Santa Claus Is Comin' To Town
12

When Santa Got Stuck Up The Chimney
15

While Shepherds Watched
18

Silent Night
20

Ding Dong Merrily On High
22

Saviour's Day
24

Deck The Hall
28

Happy Xmas (War Is Over)
30

RISE UP SHEPHERD

Traditional
Arranged by David Gedge

With a swing

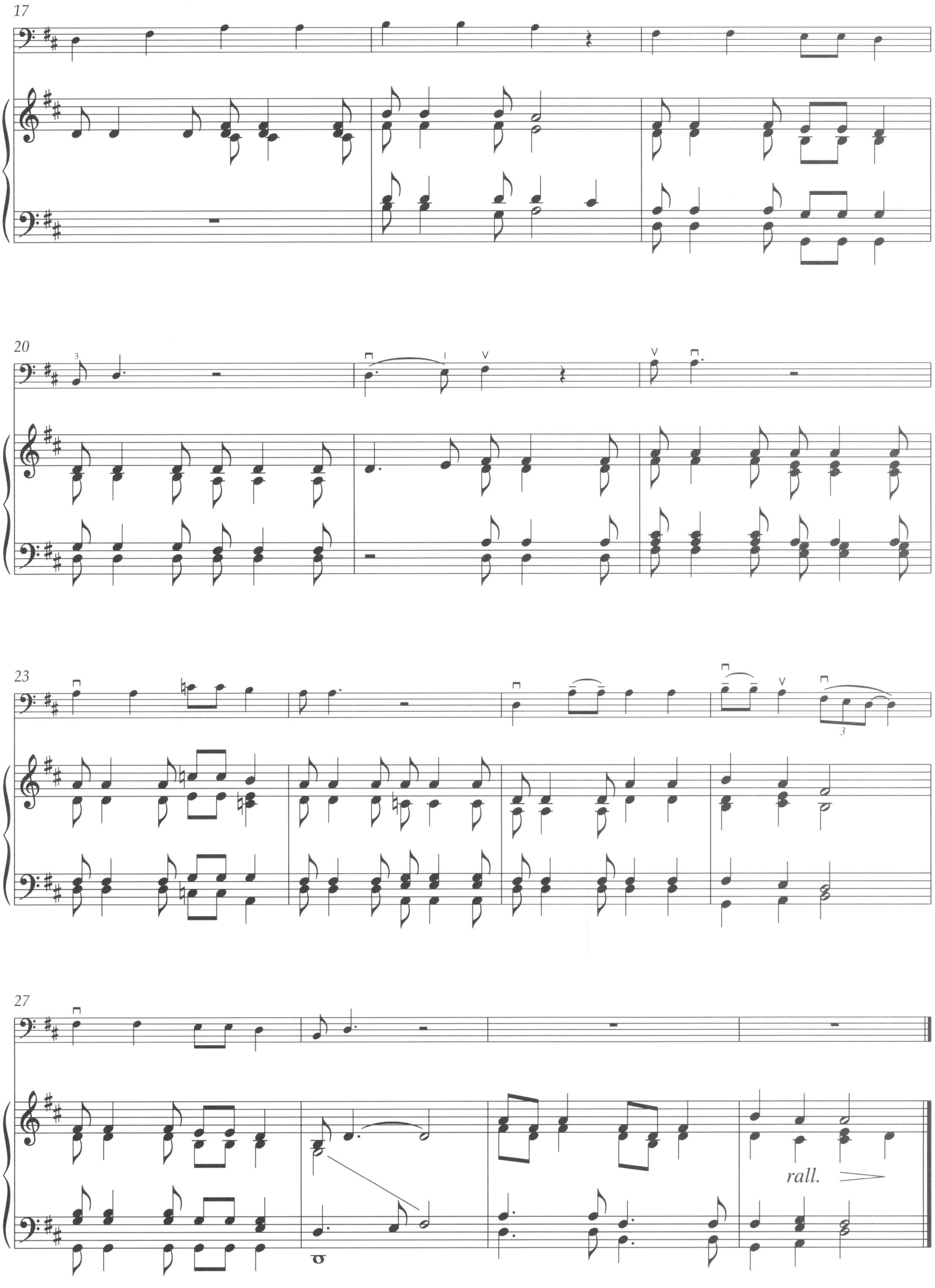
17
20
23
27
rall.

AWAY IN A MANGER

Traditional
Arranged by David Gedge

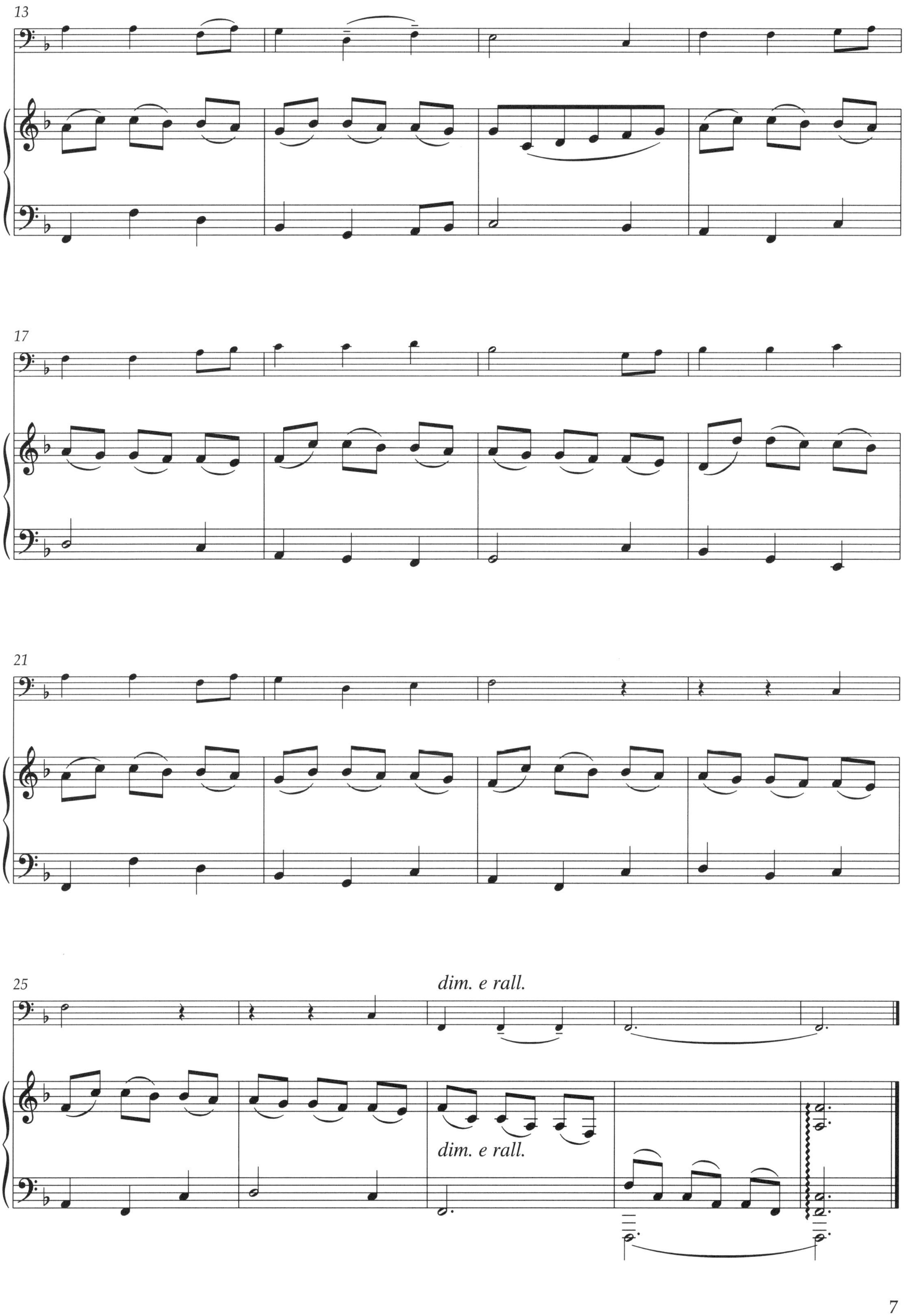
13
17
21
25
dim. e rall.
dim. e rall.

MISTLETOE AND WINE

Words by Leslie Stewart & Jeremy Paul
Music by Keith Strachan

Arranged by David Gedge

17
f
cresc.
f
Ped.
23
sim.
Ped.
29
Ped.
sim.
35
dim. e rall.
pizz.
mf
3
mf
dim. e rall.

O CHRISTMAS TREE

Traditional
Arranged by David Gedge

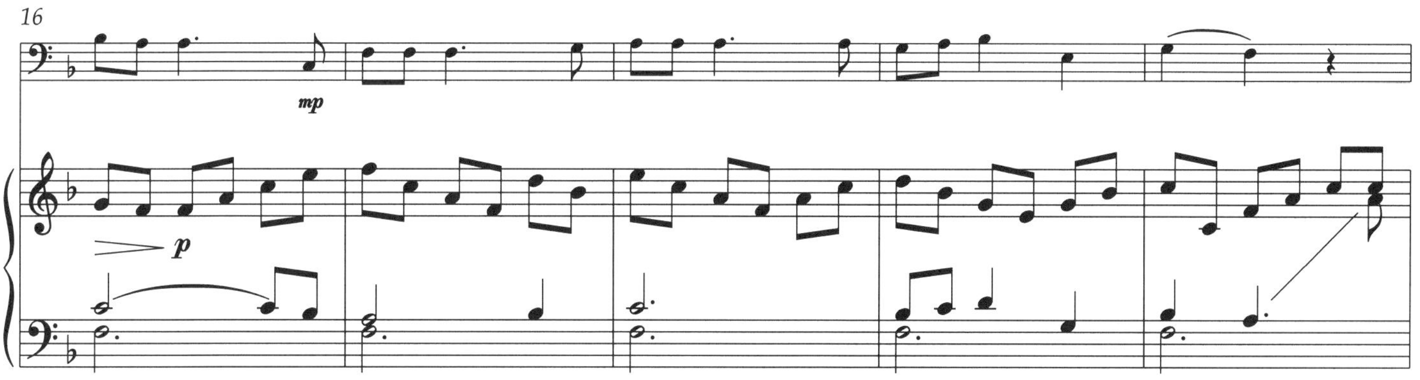
16
mp
p

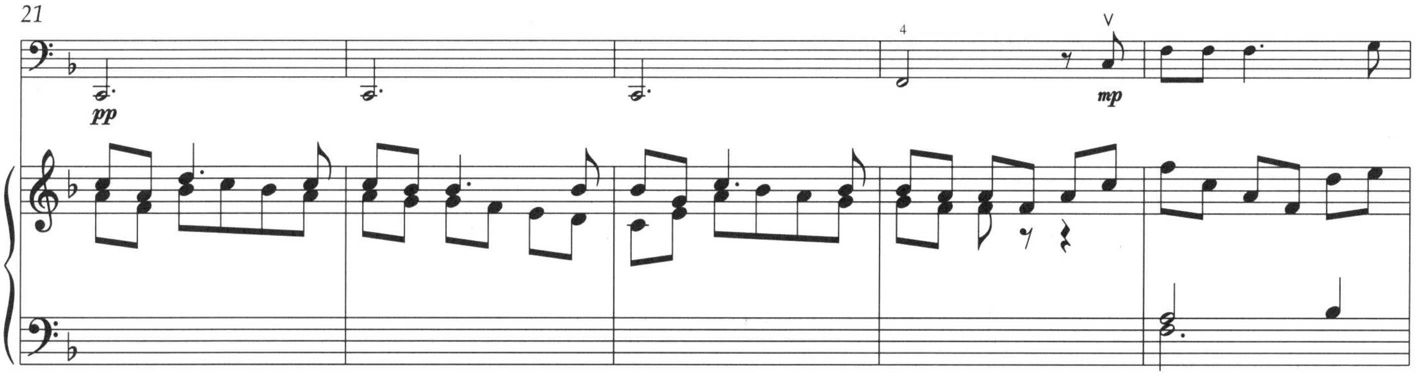
21
pp
4
mp

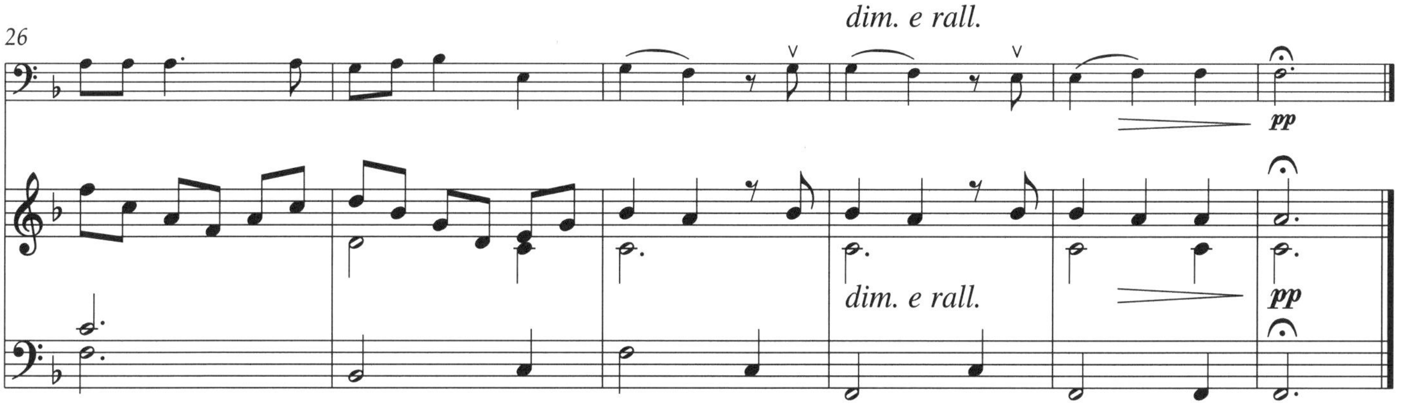
dim. e rall.
26
pp
dim. e rall.
pp

SANTA CLAUS IS COMIN' TO TOWN

Words & Music by Haven Gillespie & J. Fred Coots

Arranged by David Gedge

13

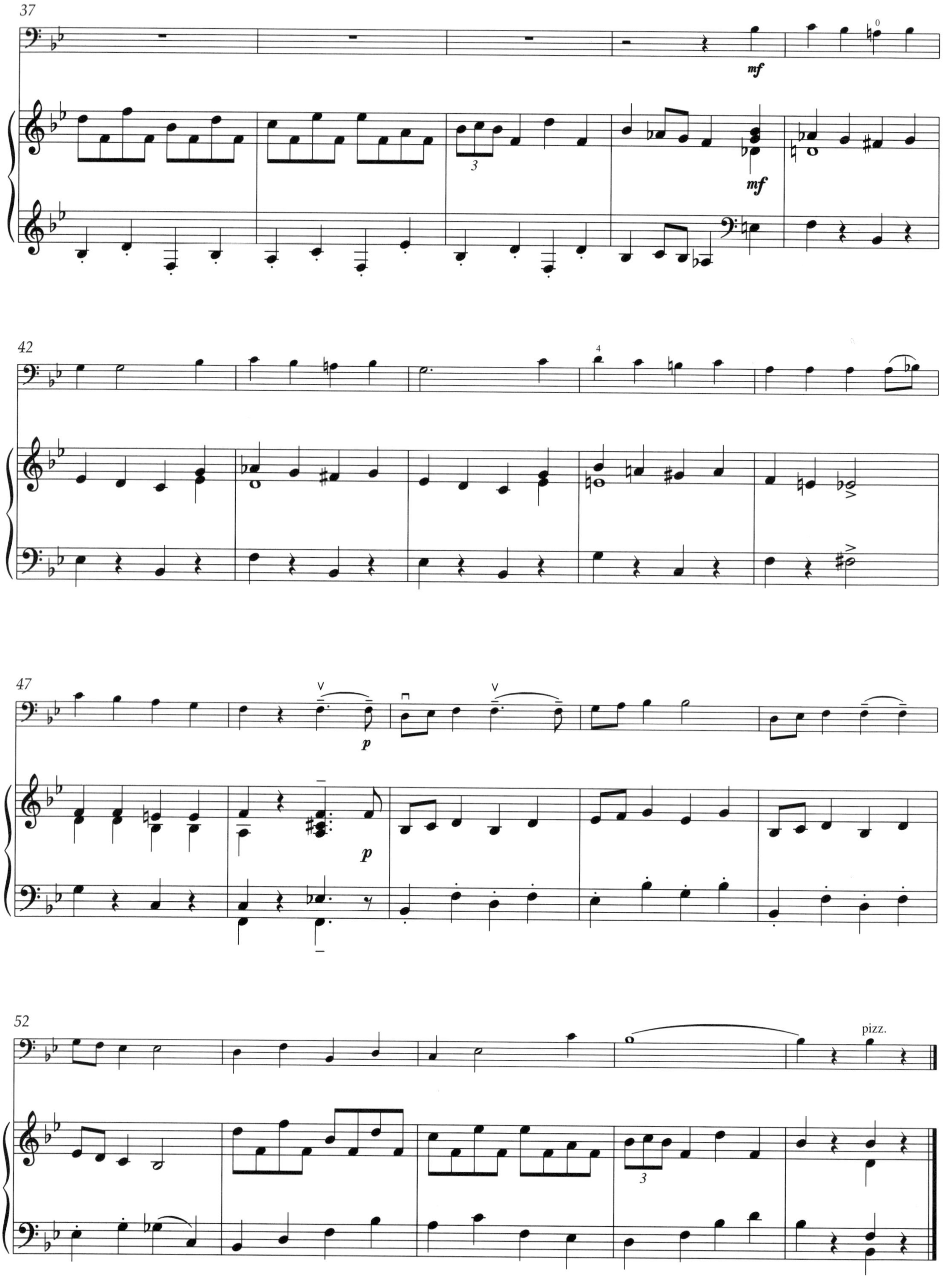
37
mf
mf
42
47
p
p
52
pizz.

WHEN SANTA GOT STUCK UP THE CHIMNEY

Words & Music by Jimmy Grafton
Arranged by David Gedge

Very steadily (not fast)

© Copyright 1953 Peermusic (UK) Limited, 8-14 Verulam Street, London WC1.
All Rights Reserved. International Copyright Secured.

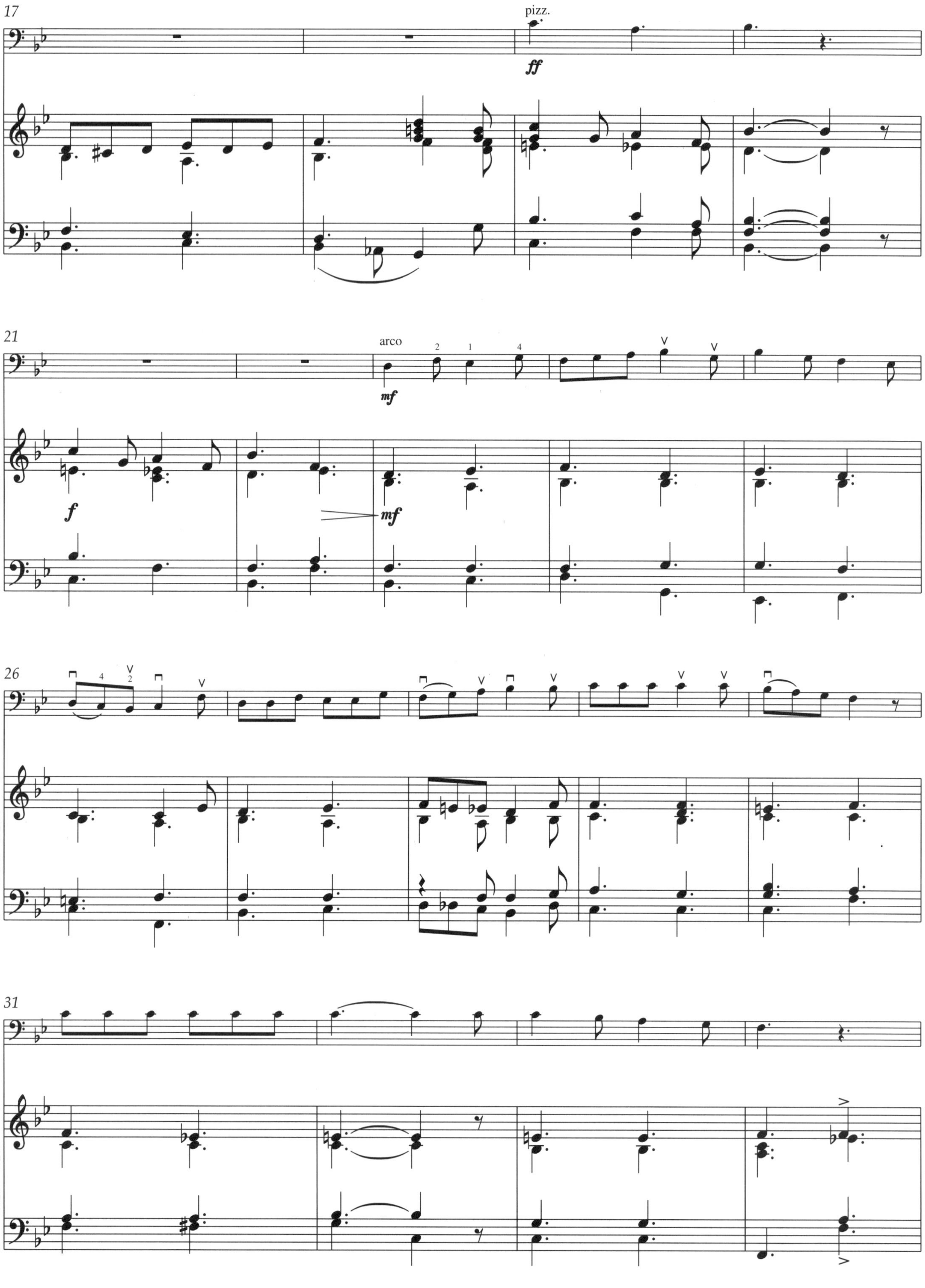
17
pizz.
ff
21
arco
mf
f
mf
26
31

17

WHILE SHEPHERDS WATCHED

Traditional
Arranged by David Gedge

Moderato

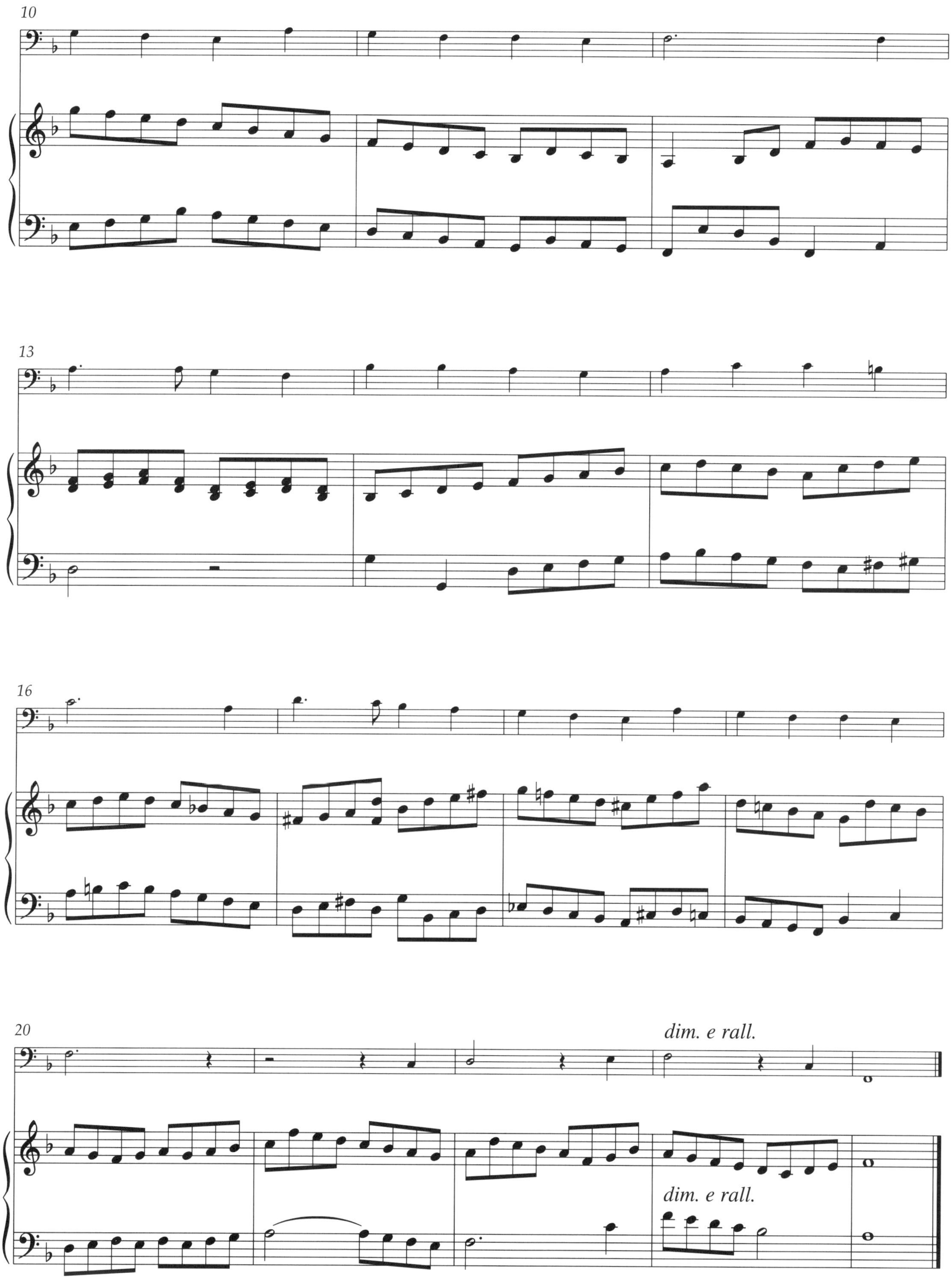
10
13
16
20
dim. e rall.
dim. e rall.

SILENT NIGHT

Music by Franz Grüber, words by Joseph Mohr

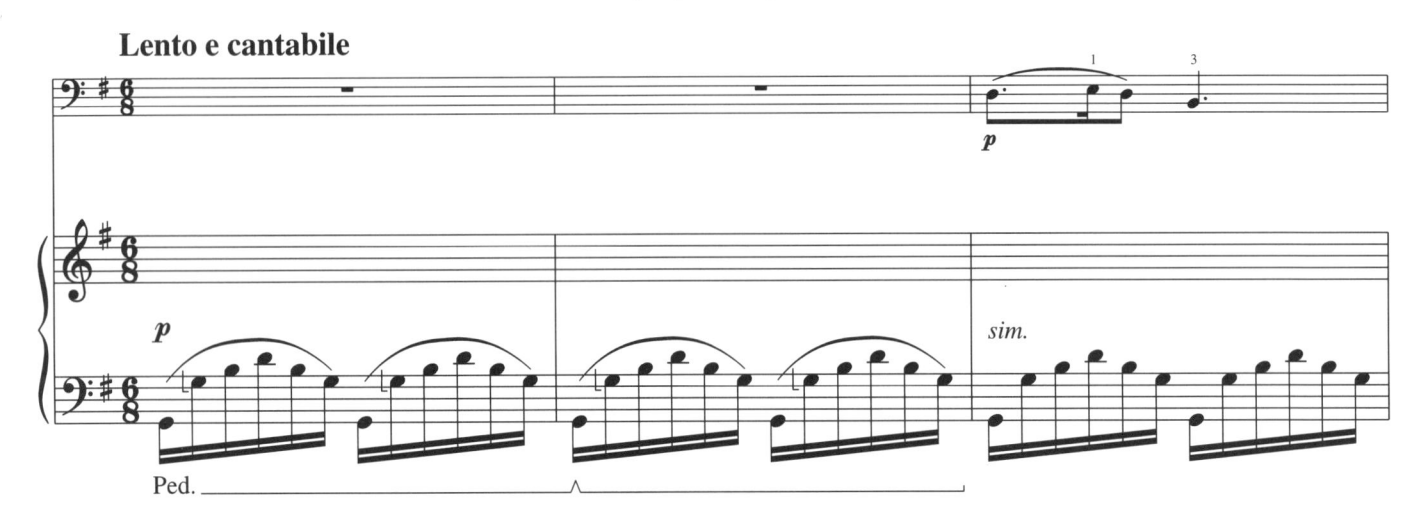

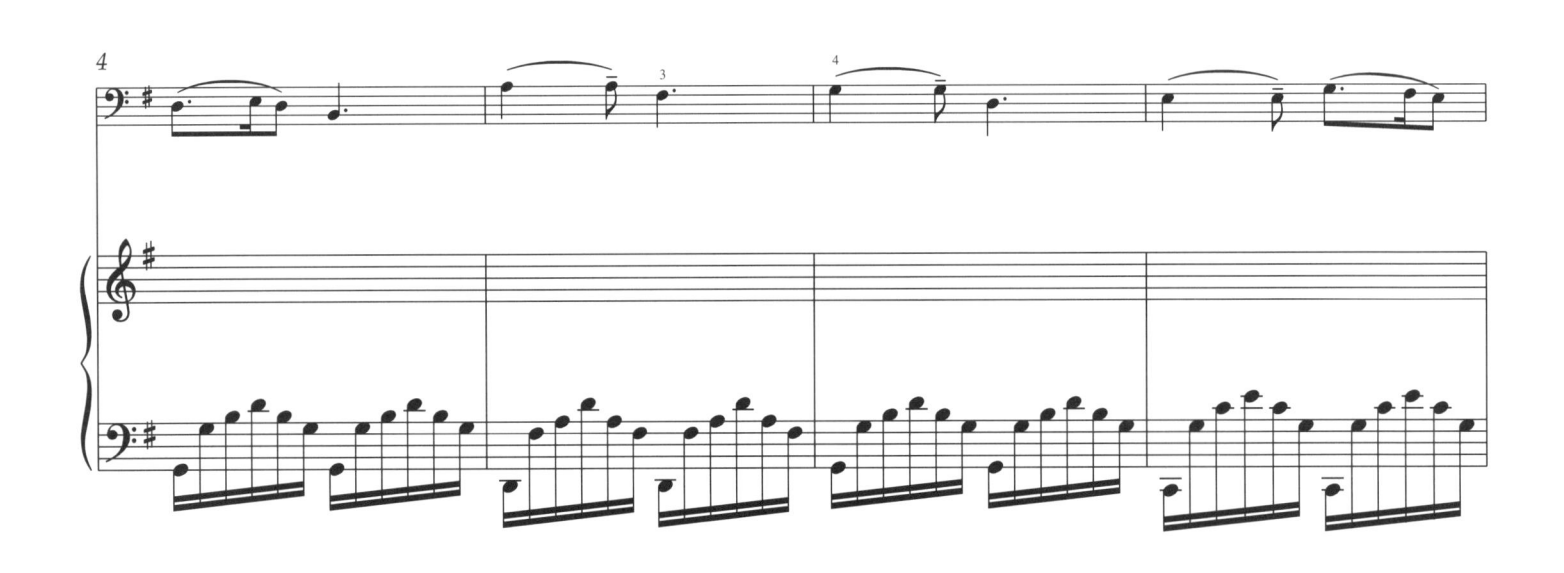

Arranged by David Gedge

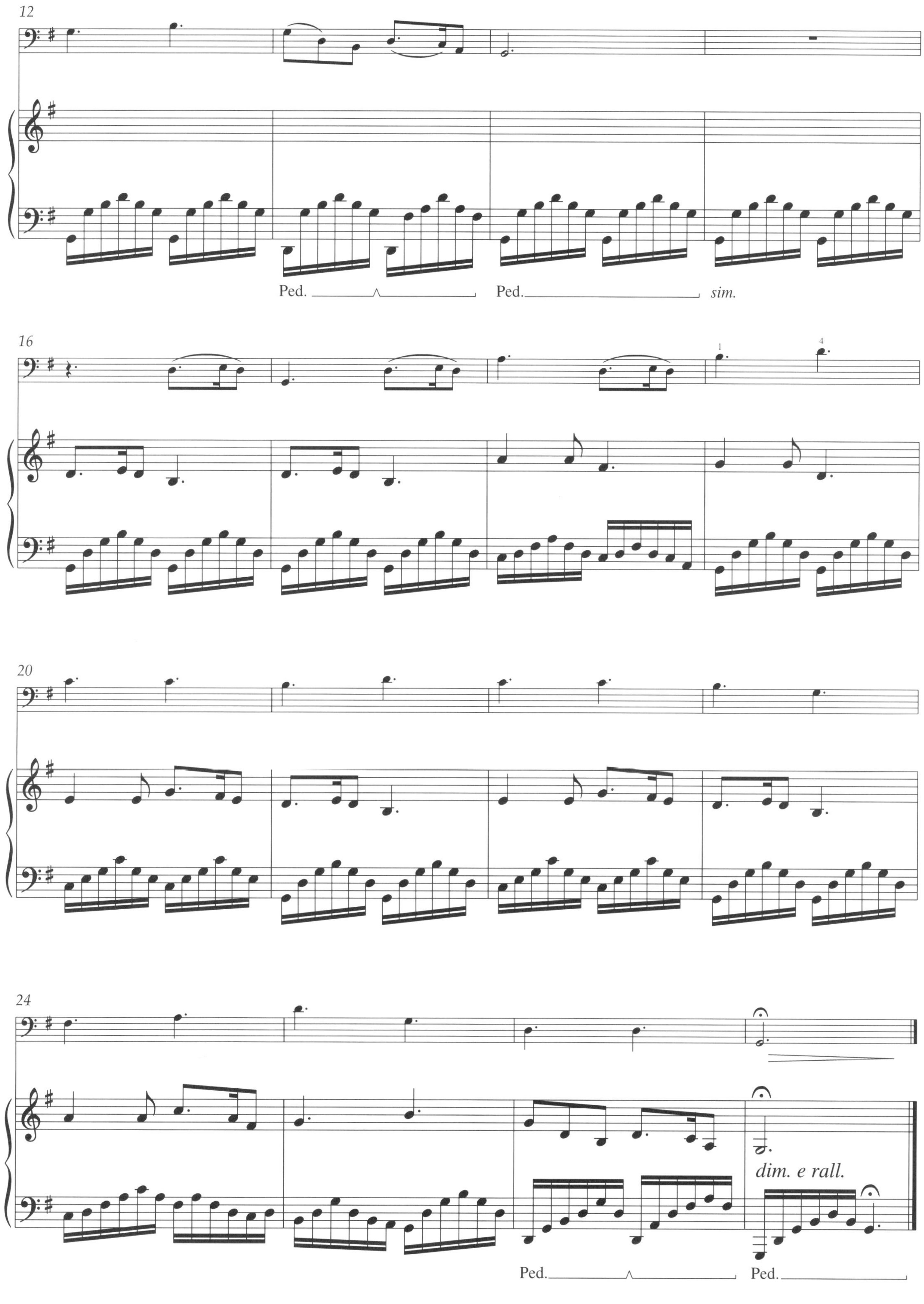
12
Ped.
Ped.
sim.
16
20
24
dim. e rall.
Ped.
Ped.

DING DONG MERRILY ON HIGH

Traditional
Arranged by David Gedge

Moderato - don't hurry

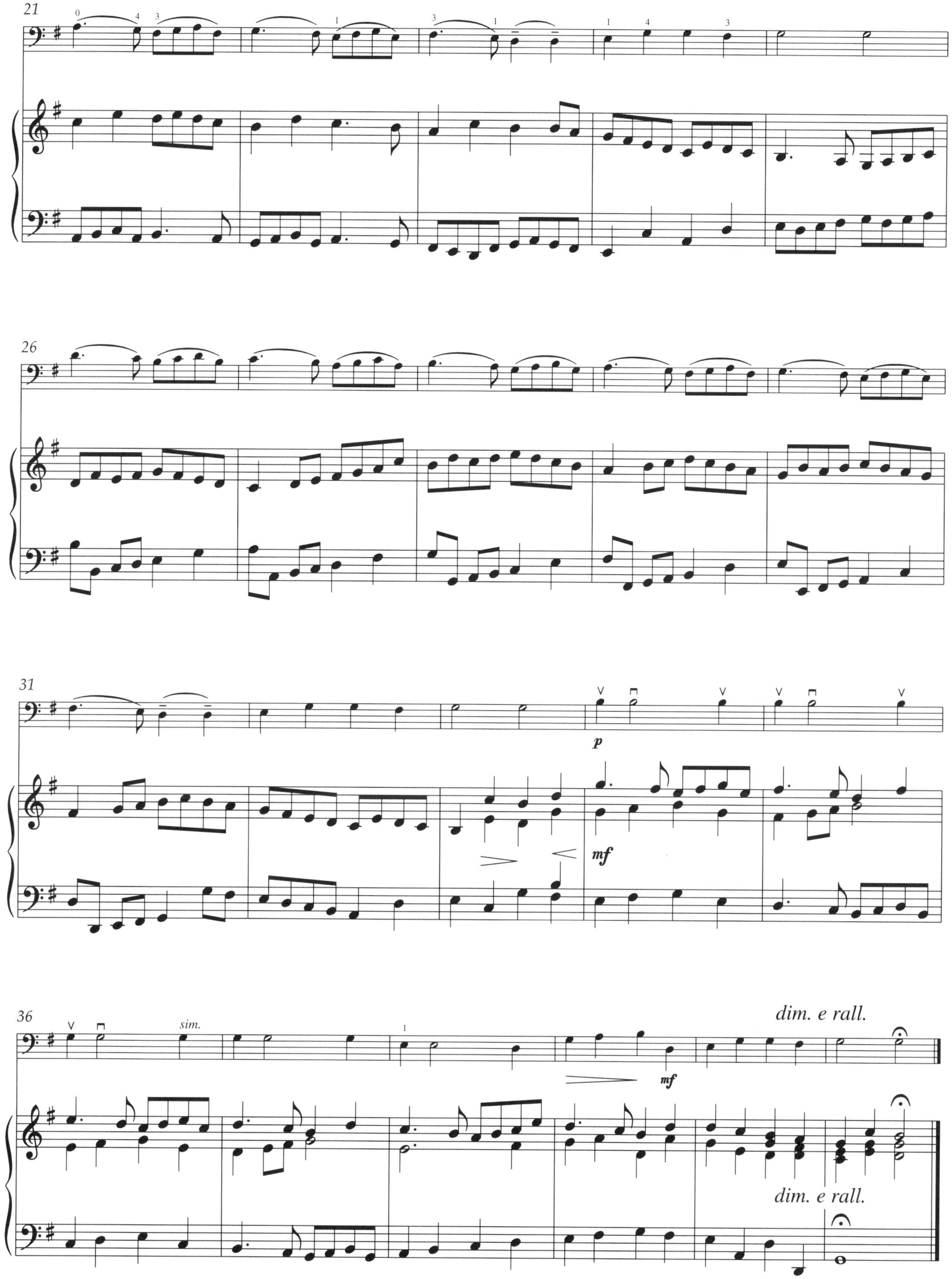
21
26
31
36
sim.
dim. e rall.
dim. e rall.

SAVIOUR'S DAY

Words & Music by Chris Eaton
Arranged by David Gedge

© Copyright 1990 Clouseau Music / SGO Music Publishing Limited, PO Box 26022, London SW10 0FY.
All Rights Reserved. International Copyright Secured.

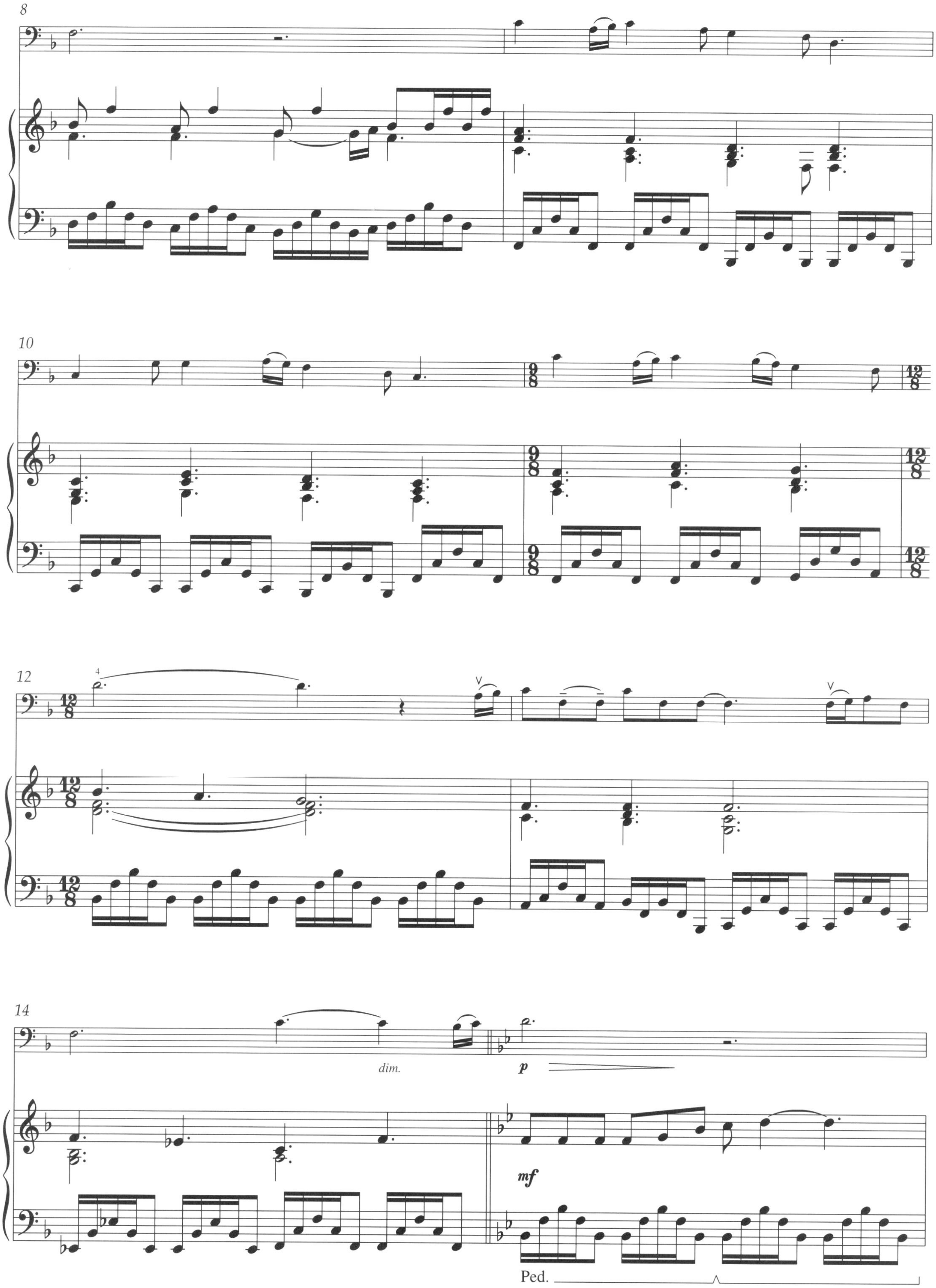
8
10
12
14
dim.
p
mf
Ped.

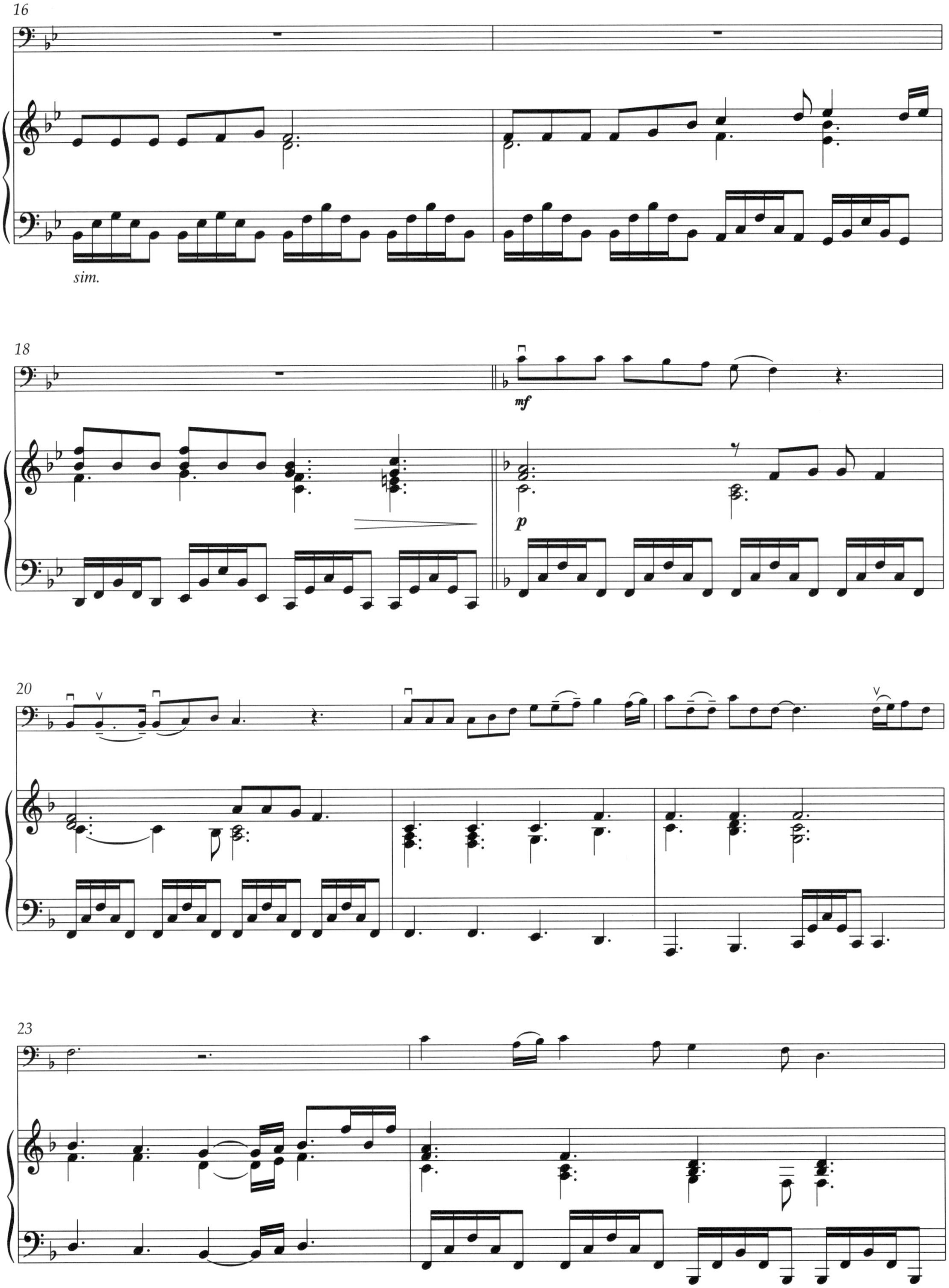
16
sim.
18
mf
p
20
23

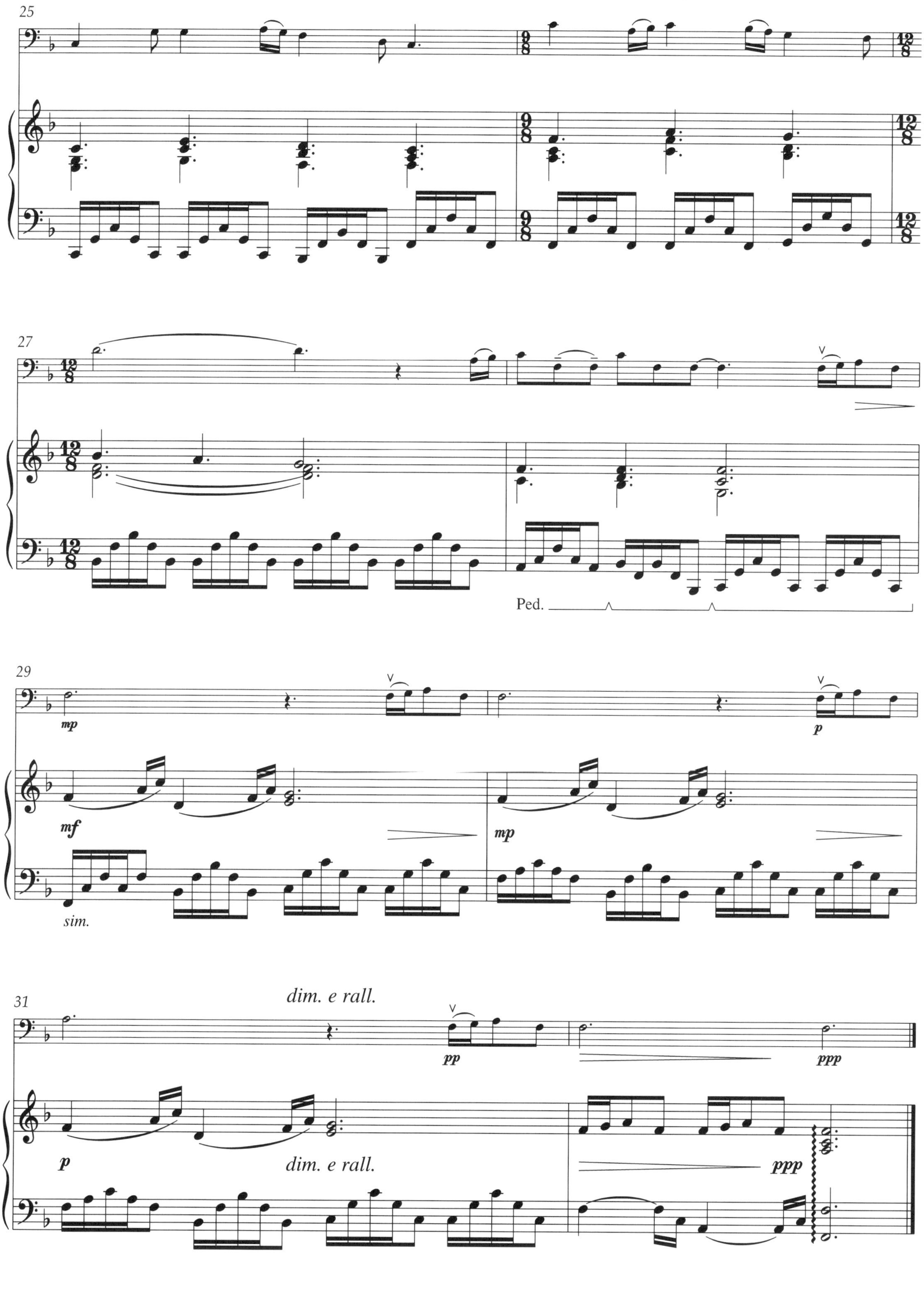
25
27
Ped.
29
mp
mf
p
mp
sim.
31
dim. e rall.
pp
ppp
p
dim. e rall.
ppp

DECK THE HALL

Nos Galan
Traditional Welsh Carol
Arranged by David Gedge

Giocoso - jolly!

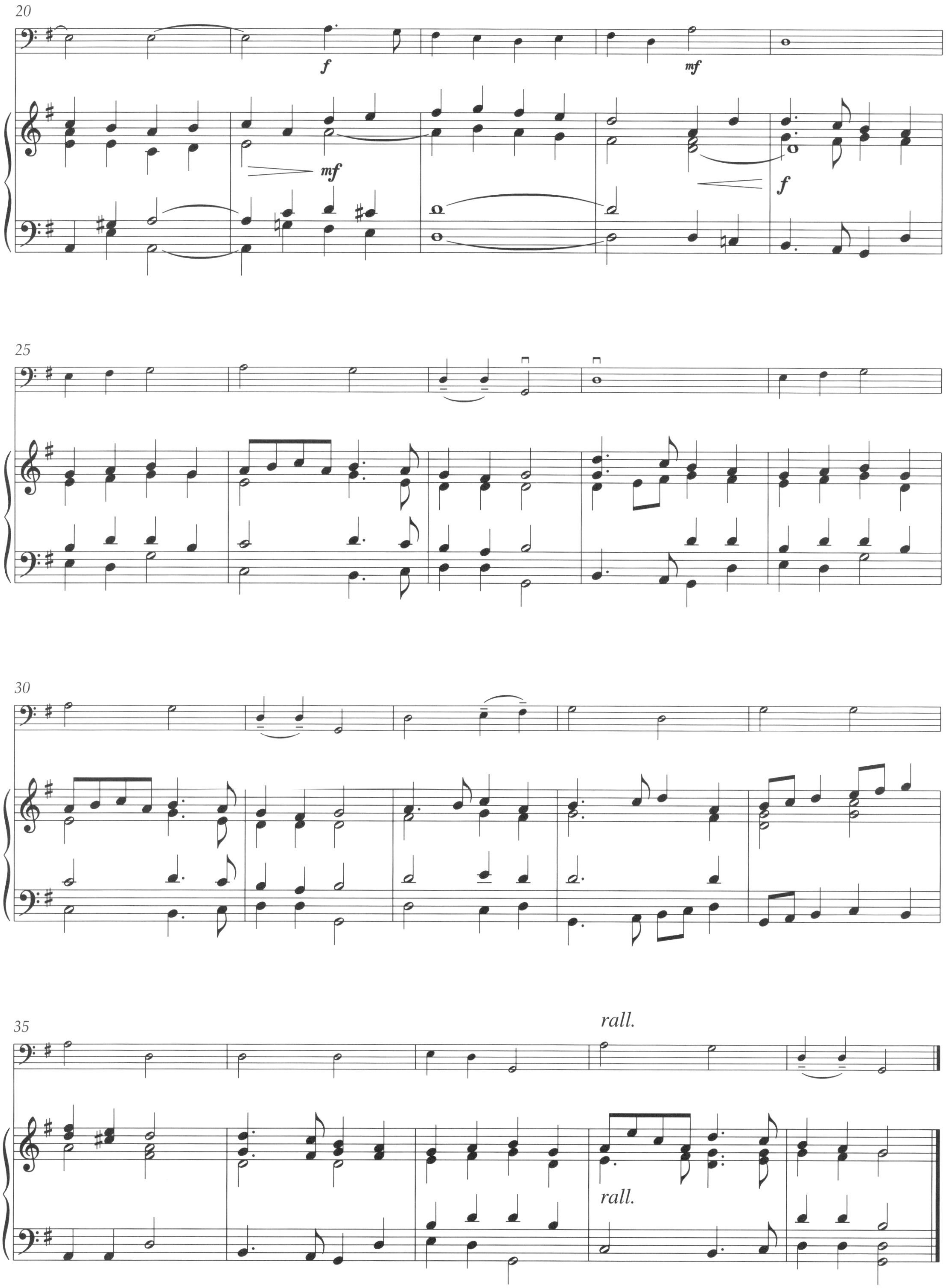
20
f
mf
mf
f
25
30
35
rall.
rall.

HAPPY XMAS (WAR IS OVER)

Words & Music by John Lennon & Yoko Ono

Arranged by David Gedge

Grazioso

© Copyright 1971 Lenono Music.
All Rights Reserved. International Copyright Secured.

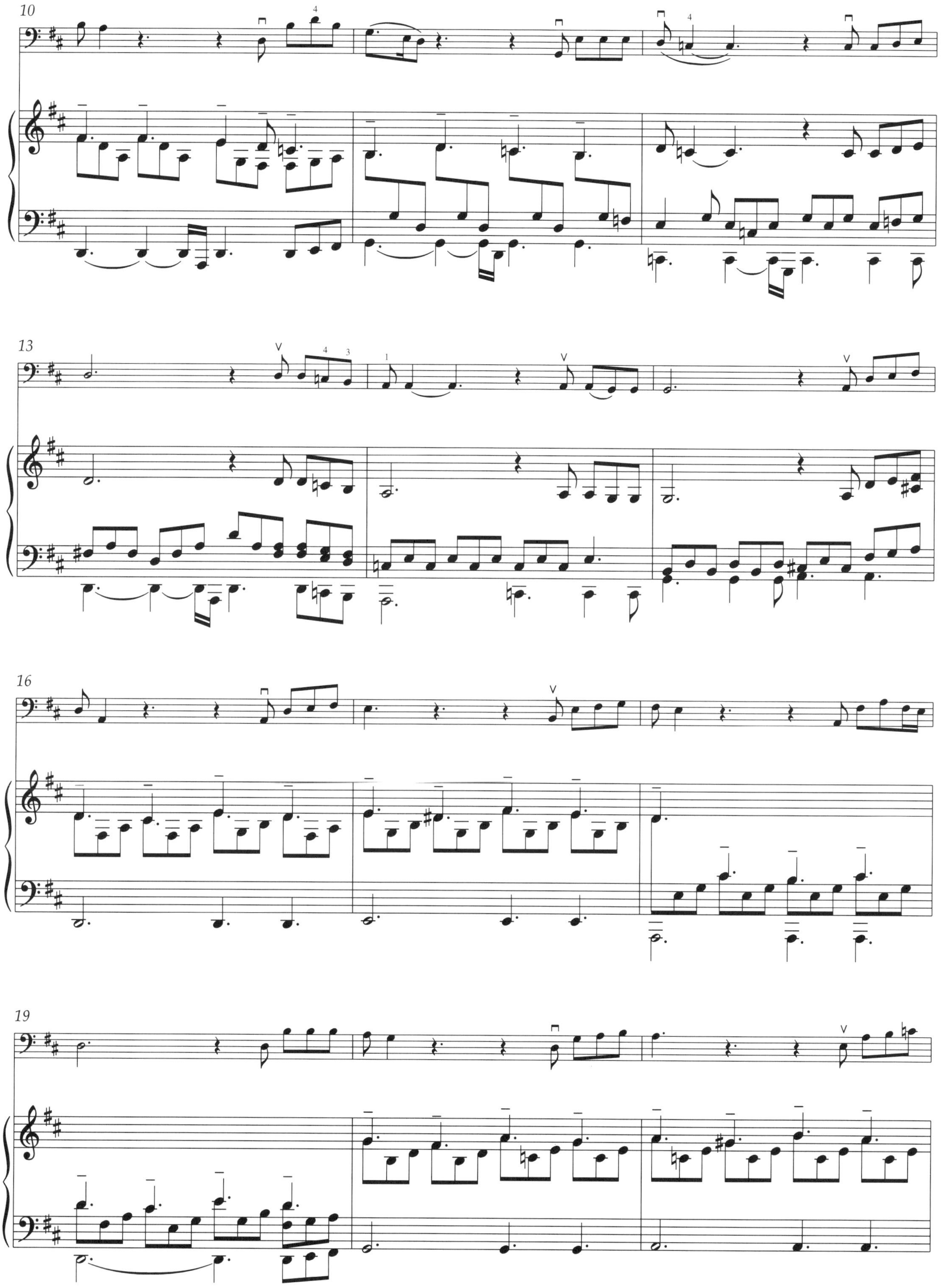
10
13
16
19

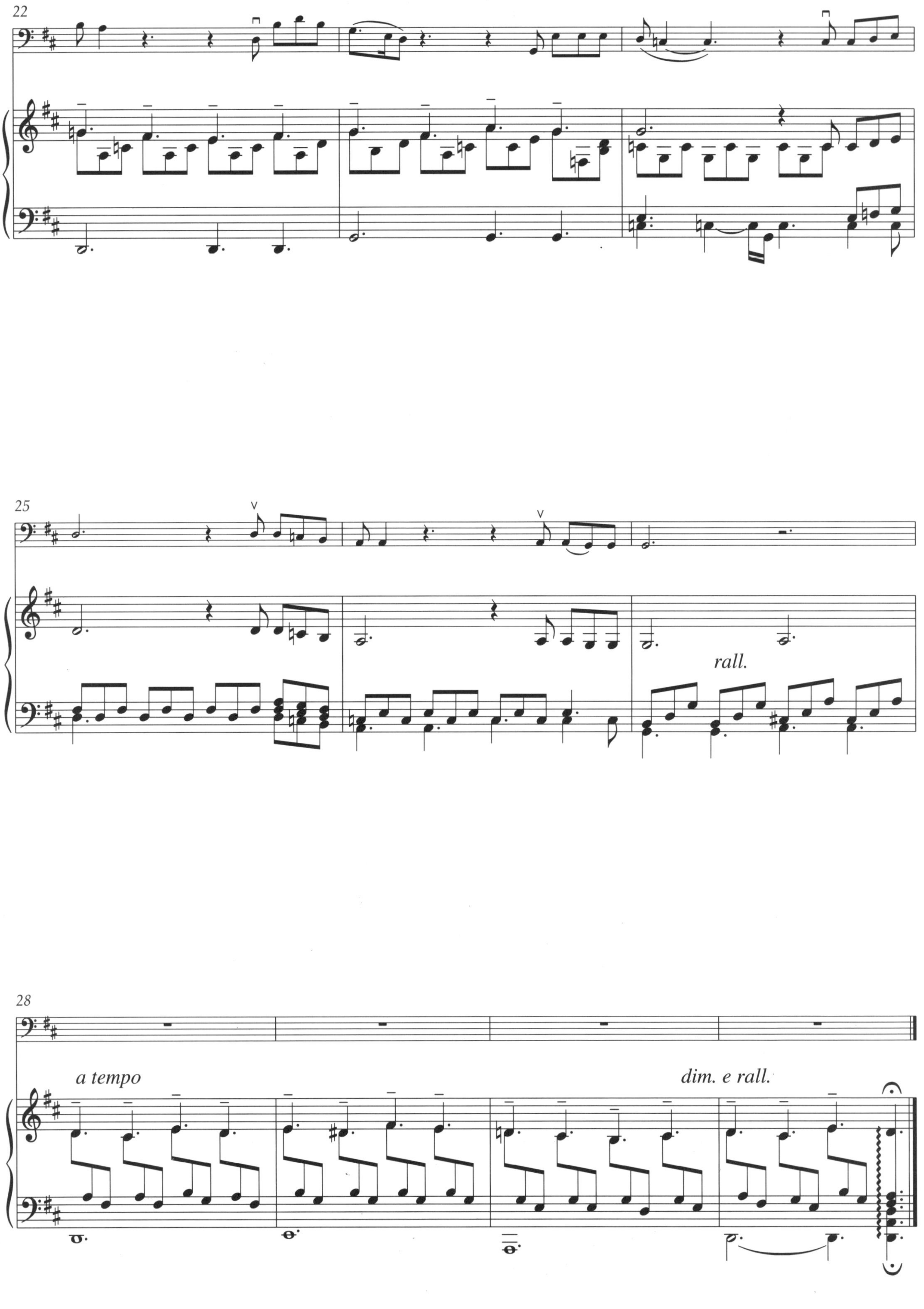
22
25
rall.
28
a tempo
dim. e rall.